NATIONAL THEATRE OF SCOTLAND

The National Theatre of Scotland was established in 2006 and has created over 200 productions. Being a theatre without walls and building-free, the Company presents a wide variety of work that ranges from largescale productions to projects tailored to the smallest performing spaces. In addition to conventional theatres, the Company has performed in airports, schools, tower blocks, community halls, ferries and forests.

The Company has toured extensively across Scotland, the rest of the UK and worldwide. Notable productions include *Black Watch* by Gregory Burke which won four Olivier Awards amongst a multitude of awards, the award-winning landmark historical trilogy *The James Plays* by Rona Munro, a radical reimagining of *Macbeth* starring Alan Cumming, presented in Glasgow and at the Lincoln Center Festival and subsequently, Broadway, New York and the Olivier Award winning *Our Ladies of Perpetual Succour*, adapted by Lee Hall from Alan Warner's novel *The Sopranos*.

The National Theatre of Scotland creates much of its work in partnership with theatre-makers, companies, venues and participants across the globe. From extraordinary projects with schools and communities, to the groundbreaking online *5 Minute Theatre* to immersive pieces such as David Greig's *The Strange Undoing of Prudencia Hart*, the National Theatre of Scotland's aspiration is to tell the stories that need to be told and to take work to wherever audiences are to be found.

Artistic Director and Chief Executive: **Jackie Wylie**
Chair: **Seona Reid DBE**
For the latest information on all our activities, visit us online at
nationaltheatrescotland.com

Scottish Government
Riaghaltas na h-Alba

National Theatre of Scotland presents

E V E

Written by Jo Clifford & Chris Goode
Directed by Susan Worsfold

Cast

Jo Clifford

Creative Team

Chris Goode	Co-Writer
Jo Clifford	Co-Writer
Susan Worsfold	Director
Susan Worsfold	Set Designer
Chris Goode	Composer
Kai Fisher	Lighting Designer
Matt Padden	Sound Designer
Seth Hardwick	Projection Designer
Aileen Sherry	Costume Designer

Production Team

Fiona Fraser	Production Manager
Lee Davis	Company Stage Manager
Anne Page	Deputy Stage Manager
Emma Yeomans	Deputy Stage Manager
Andy Gannon	Technical Manager
Andy Reid	Production Video

Jo Clifford & Chris Goode

EVE

OBERON BOOKS
LONDON

WWW.OBERONBOOKS.COM

First published in 2017 by Oberon Books Ltd
521 Caledonian Road, London N7 9RH
Tel: +44 (0) 20 7607 3637 / Fax: +44 (0) 20 7607 3629
e-mail: info@oberonbooks.com
www.oberonbooks.com

A catalogue record for this book is available from the British
Library.

PB ISBN: 9781786822697
E ISBN: 9781786822703

Cover photograph by Christopher Bowen

Photo credits: Rebecca Innes, Neil Montgomery, Mark Bunyan;
Thurston Hopkins/Picture Post/Hulton Archive/Getty Images

Printed, bound and converted
by CPI Group (UK) Ltd, Croydon, CR0 4YY.

Visit www.oberonbooks.com to read more about all our books
and to buy them. You will also find features, author interviews and
news of any author events, and you can sign up for e-newsletters
so that you're always first to hear about our new releases.

Preface

I have been thinking about my life.
I've been looking through the photographs.
I have been making a list. A list of everything that happened.

That's how this play began. Me and Chris Goode in a rehearsal room with a heap of photographs and a steadily expanding timeline snaking its way across a wall.

Part of what we listed was representations I saw of who I am.

The pantomime dame that made me look ridiculous.
The murderer in *Psycho* who made me look like a sick criminal.
The beautiful young Dietrich impersonator in *The Damned* who made me into an embodiment of evil.

And then nothing for years and years. Telling me I did not exist.

I took all this personally when I was young because I had no defences against it. And no alternative sources of information.

Being a child in the fifties meant there was nothing at all. Words like "transgender" did not even exist.

I felt as if I was something unspeakable. And completely alone.

I was in my forties when *The Crying Game* came out. And for the first time in my life I saw a trans character being played by a trans actress. And portrayed as a loving worthwhile person.

But even then when the hero discovers she was born male he slaps her hard and runs off to vomit.

So *EVE* is above all an act of resistance. Of resistance against hatred and against fear and against shame.

I could have fictionalised my experiences; but I chose not to because open pride is the best way to resist shame.

When I began to live as a woman there was a huge emphasis on 'passing'. I was given voice lessons so I could sound like a woman and encouraged to learn to walk and sit like a woman. The assumption being that people would hate and despise me if they discovered I was trans.

And the abuse I suffered in those early days when I went out my front door and the hatred I provoked when I performed my *Gospel According to Jesus Queen Of Heaven* seemed to confirm the good sense of this.

But it also made it all the more important to resist.

I'm lucky to live in Scotland where my existence is protected by law, and that means, I think, that I have a duty to live openly and not conceal who I am.

Because that in itself is an act of resistance.

There are so many places in this world where we cannot live openly. Where to do so puts us in grave danger of torture and death.

I want to dedicate the play to my sisters and brothers who live in such places.

And to everyone everywhere struggling to become their own dear selves and live free from fear and from shame.

Jo Clifford

PART ONE

1.

This all began when I was a child —

when I looked in the mirror and saw a boy

and didn't really know who he was.

And that made me so afraid.

I was very young then. Maybe four or five.
But old enough to know I could tell no one.

Old enough to know it was too dangerous to say.

It's not true what they tell you, that children don't know their own minds.

I knew. I just couldn't give it a name.

Today I want to write a manifesto.

I want to write a manifesto because I feel militant.

Because I have been thinking about my life.

I've been looking through the photographs.

I have been making a list. A list of everything that happened.

I've been writing it all down.

This is when they sent me away.

This is when my mum died.

This is when I thought it was all my fault.

This is when no one spoke to me for months and months.

This is when I thought no one would ever love me.

This is when I wanted to die.

This is when Lorca taught me not to die and I went to Spain.

This is when I ate yoghurt for the very first time.

But at first there was nothing. It was like I didn't exist.

My dad used to watch the boxing

and sometimes he'd let me watch it too, as a special treat.

I'd keep my eyes tight shut and listen to the commentator

because in spite of everything his voice was kind.

Shortly after my mum died

I got taken to the pantomime.

My first ever trip to the theatre.

I saw Billy Dainty as Widow Twankey in Aladdin. He was dressed as a ballerina — I don't know why.

He did a striptease right down to his underwear.

Everybody laughed at him. What he did

could have been beautiful.

I wanted to be Princess Jasmine

who wore the most beautiful dresses.

But I must have known, somehow, deep inside:

known I was Widow Twankey

and that meant everyone would laugh at me.

My dad liked to watch the Black and White Minstrel Show.

I wanted to be one of the chorus girls

and have long legs in tights and wear a sparkly leotard and on the top of my head, a plume

and dance in high heels and always keep smiling.

But I couldn't do that could I?

I wasn't even supposed to think that was I?

Being a boy.

But don't think I'm going to tell you a story of suffering.

A story of unhappiness and betrayal and being a victim of it all.

And I will not tell you the story of a girl born into a boy's body,

whose troubles end when she meets a nice kind surgeon who gives her a vagina.

No.

Because a girl can have a penis. A boy can have a vagina.

We all have our bodies.

I've come here to tell you the story of a child.

A child who was frightened and angry.

A child who was lied to throughout their young life.

But who became someone beautiful:

the beautiful person they were all along.

I want the story I tell to spread hope

and communicate gratitude for the beauty and courage

and the riches we bring to the world.

And I know where I want to begin.

2.

Just look at this boy.

This boy looking out at me with bewildered eyes

This boy looking out at me

This boy who loves music

Loves music more than anything in the world

Except perhaps his mother

Look how much he loves the music on his Pixiephone

Look.

The Fascination of Youth

Reproduced by kind permission of "Picture Post"

And here he is again.

The picture of boyhood.

Look at him — five, maybe six, in his woolly socks and his Start Rite shoes.

His hair cut short

and his old dark coat

standing in the stern of his father's boat

watching the train.

Exactly what a boy should be.

Robert John

with his photo in Picture Post:

'The Fascination of Youth.'

I was a star from a very early age.

I didn't know this! I was told I was a problem.

But you can tell the photographer knows I'm a star.

I loved the train and I loved the boat.

On the boat I felt safe and I loved being me.

Funny how on the boat it didn't seem to matter, being a boy.

I've been chosen to represent boyhood

but really it's me-hood.

3.

Look how alone this boy is.

He's been sent away to be made a man.

Sent away from his mother.

Because everyone knows

it's bad for a growing boy to be too close to his mother.

The dormitories are all named after famous generals

and the beds are made of iron

and the blankets are all grey

and there's rugby every winter afternoon

and whatever happens you must never ever cry.

And the music room is also used for boxing.

And the time comes they put boxing gloves on him

and they put him in the ring.

His opponent is a red-haired boy called Cousins

who everyone says is the best boxer in the school.

The boy puts up his hands, as he's supposed to.

But he can't fight. Instead he

bursts into tears

and everyone is watching

and Cousins says: "Hit me. Please."

But he can't. He can't hit Cousins.

There must be something terribly wrong.

What's wrong? What's wrong with the boy?

Look there's the music teacher.

Mr Fowler. Always so cross. He'd play a bit of music and tell the boys what to think.

He'd say, the saxophone isn't a proper instrument, and jazz isn't music,

and he'd make us sing 'Dashing Away With The Smoothing Iron'

and 'Loch Lomond' sometimes —

the high road and the low road

and me and my true love would never meet again, for some reason.

It must have been very sad.

He'd get all the new boys to sing.

He'd call us up one by one and make us stand beside him by the piano and sing.

He played 'Three Blind Mice' and the boy was supposed to sing it back.

And I couldn't. I just couldn't somehow.

So when the school did *HMS Pinafore*

I was given a plain gingham dress and was one of the sisters and the cousins and the aunts.

and I would open and shut my mouth vaguely in time to the music.

But Cousins was the Captain's daughter, Josephine,

And got to wear the most beautiful crinoline.

So there's the boy.

The boy who can't fight

and who can't sing

and so who never sings.

Songs go round and round inside his head

and there is no way for them to come out.

And I'm looking at the boy.

The boy who lost his voice.

He cannot stop this story

He cannot stop this story running in his head

Because he has lost his voice for ever.

Darkness.

4.

They called it a preparatory school

Because it was supposed to prepare you —

Prepare you for this.

But nothing can prepare you for this.

I can't call you John any more.

John is no longer your name,

because in that place no one ever uses Christian names.

I have to call you Clifford.

Clifford has to wear army uniform, polish army boots,

and march up and down on Monday afternoons

being shouted at by sergeants.

Each day he walks under an arch with all the names on it

The names engraved in stone

The names of the young men murdered in both the world wars

And walk past the statue of the famous general Haig

Who sent those young men to their deaths.

Clifford's being groomed

— to do the same.

You so long to be a normal boy

You know somehow that you aren't

You know somehow that you never will be

You boy with the round shoulders and the beginnings of a stoop

The boy convinced his penis is smaller than everyone else's

Who can't bear for it to be seen because it's missing something

— something he can't talk about.

O my love what's missing is your foreskin:

you were circumcised at birth.

But no one thought to tell you that.

So right now it's all part of the big terrible thing that somehow

Somehow makes you not a proper boy.

This big terrible thing you can never talk about

that makes you completely alone.

I can't tell anybody anything

— not even that I want to be a famous writer.

I can't tell anyone that because they'll laugh and if they laugh
I'll die because it's all that keeps me alive and all the things
I'm going to write —

they burn in me like fire.

When I look at this picture I see you unloved and frightened
and so deeply hurt.

But my friend sees fierceness and courage and resolve.

A fierce sense of you-ness in spite of everything.

And it's that that's enabled me to live.

That's what kept us both alive.

I owe my life to you and my success.

All those dreams you had that seemed so impossible have all
come true.

Darkness.

5.

The room's so hot.

The boy's dad is looking so sad

Sitting in an armchair by a roaring fire

The boy thinks: What have I done wrong? And in his hand he has a letter from his mum

It says: Show you're pleased to see daddy

So he tries. The boy tries to give his dad a little smile

But his dad does not smile back

They sit the boy down far too close to the fire

And the dad says: Mummy's been ill. Mummy's been so very ill

So very very ill that she's died.

And the boy thinks that's impossible I only saw her yesterday.

The boy is twelve years old

His mum had come down to visit him at school as a special treat

And it was all so lovely

But there's a kind of darkness in the father's eye

And the boy knows that this is happening

Only he can't feel it somehow, as if it's happening to someone else

Only it's happening to him.

They go out for a walk. It's so cold.

They have a cream tea

and then they go back to the school

with its dormitories named after famous generals

and the father leaves his son there

in Montgomery.

And it's me. It's my dad. My mum. Me.

And I know now

when the really bad things happen you have to deal with them alone.

Darkness.

6.

Hello John

— I'll call you John because your true friends called you John

All two of them, who kept you alive

And me also. I am your true friend

And I was always with you, somewhere.

They had no idea, did they?

They had no fucking idea what they were doing

And you think it's all your fault

But it's not

It's not your fault

It never was

And there you are my loved one

The actress. You were Sylvia in *One Way Pendulum*

and you were Lizzie in *Next Time I'll Sing To You*

and they made you feel so alive

Lizzie and Sylvia

They gave you a place in the world

But because it was too dangerous to show the woman inside you

you lost that place as soon as you had found it

and theatre became a place of fear and shame.

It's taken fifty years for you to find your way home.

PART TWO

1.

I'm grown up now. I'm in a restaurant.

A restaurant called Luigi's.

I hesitated before I came in.

I always hesitate before I come in.

It's quite nice really.

A man comes up to me, doing the handsome Italian thing

— maybe it's Luigi.

And he calls me madam without any visible effort at all.

He brings me the menu and a glass of good red wine and

it's maybe silly of me to say this, Luigi,

but you don't know

You don't know how much this means to me.

You're maybe out the back gossiping about me

but please don't let me see that.

Luigi, once upon a time I had to see a gender specialist

—they're the gatekeepers, Luigi,

that hold the keys to the life we need to live.

My specialist always wore pretty dresses that were cut just a
little bit too short.

The unspoken expectation was that whenever I saw her

I had to wear something feminine too.

Because she wasn't there to listen to me really or pay attention to what I needed.

She was there to see if I was a true transsexual

and if she decided I wasn't

she was there to weed me out.

I had a dear friend who was an expert in town planning.

She was too afraid to wear a dress,

and so she was considered not to be serious

and was struck off the specialist's list.

Which is why I always wore a skirt,

though I didn't always want to,

and a wig that was held on by hair clips

and heavy make-up to conceal my facial hair.

The clinic was right at the end of a bus route

and people can be so vile on buses —

and then when I got off at the end I'd have to walk down an immensely long corridor

past all these open doors where people could see me.

Her clinic was in the same place where women came

when they were about to have their babies.

It wasn't the best place for me to be.

One day I was early and the sun was shining

And I wasn't quite ready to deal with the corridor.

So I sat in the sunshine at the edge of the car park

Expecting a crowd to gather, probably

To point at the freak and make rude remarks

And to laugh and to laugh.

But that didn't happen.

People walked past, everyone so happy to be in the sunshine.

And my body, clenched so long in fear and shame,

My body opened up to the gentle heat of the afternoon.

I knew then.

There was me in my fifties and I finally knew

Knew for the very first time

Knew I had every right to be in the world.

Does that make sense to you?

You so fortunately born into the gender that suited you

You who've always known you had a place in the world.

So thank you, Luigi, thank you for calling me madam.

Thank you for the wine. It tastes so good.

I've worked so hard for this.

This peace. This solitude.

This place where no one is shouting at me

Or talking about me

Or pointing at me

Or laughing at me

And everything is going so well.

2.

I wish I didn't need to go to the toilet.

I'm angry this still makes me anxious

but I swallow my fear and I go down the stairs

Down the stairs to the ladies.

There are places in America

Places in the land of the free

where if I did this I'd be breaking the law.

They could fine me or send me to jail.

And if one of you out there in the audience —

one of you lucky enough to be born female

and even luckier to be happy with that —

if one of you saw me there, in the ladies' loo

you'd have the right to sue this place

and seek compensation for your emotional distress.

I was in another basement once

At the very bottom of the New York Metropolitan Opera House

Where I'd gone to see Wagner's Ring Cycle

And I needed to pee

As you do in the Ring Cycle

Because it takes such a very long time for the world to come to an end.

And no one said to Wagner: Ricky, don't you think this is just a little long?

And because of that there were huge long queues to the restrooms

Only there was no rest for me because I still wore gender neutral clothes

And I didn't dare join the impossibly elegant ladies.

And in the men's, gentlemen sniggered and asked me if I was in the wrong line.

So I asked if there was a gender neutral toilet somewhere

And it took several fraught telephone conversations

Before I could be escorted down to the deepest basement in the building

Where there was a door marked 'Security'

Behind which sat a huge tough New York cop,

Who grunted,

And who, after he'd grunted, took out the most enormous bunch of keys

Reluctantly took his feet off the desk

And led me through a door marked

'Strictly Private'

And down a long strictly private corridor

To a door marked 'Medical Centre'

Which he also unlocked

And inside the medical centre was another door

Which he also unlocked

And behind that door was the only gender neutral toilet in the whole of the New York Metropolitan Opera House.

And Siegmund made love to his twin sister

And the Valkyries did their riding, because it was their job

And Wotan abandoned his disobedient daughter inside the ring of fire

And Siegfried forged his magic sword and learnt the secret language of birds

And each time I would have to be escorted down the long long strictly private corridor

But the guard would never talk to me and never look me in the eye.

It was a different guard for every journey, so I had to explain it again and again

And so it went on for days and days until the very last night of all

When Siegfried colluded in the rape of Brünnhilde and the world was finally about to end

And I went down to the basement and had to explain all over again and the man looked at me and said: No. The room's in use.

And I knew he was lying. And I looked at him and he looked at me and I saw the contempt in his eye and he said: Go to the men's.

And I had to, trying not to let anyone see my tears.

But when the lights went down in the theatre I could weep in the darkness.

Not at the downfall of the gods or Brünnhilde burning herself alive or even the death of her beautiful horse

But at my own shame and humiliation.

And that was how I experienced the high culture of America.

3.

So here I am at the door of the ladies

feeling just the tiniest bit afraid.

But it's nice here. Nice in the ladies in Luigi's.

There's a lovely mirror with curlicues

and a lovely chair that could almost belong to a copy of the palace of Versailles.

Ladies' toilets always tend to be so much nicer than gents'.

Often when you meet a lady in the ladies they smile at you and look you in the eye, and you smile back.

In a gents no one ever smiles or looks anyone in the eye.

I used to spend a lot of time waiting in gents' toilets

Waiting for the stall to be free

because I couldn't pee standing up at the trough.

Because if I tried to pee standing up it would just make me so anxious

and then I wouldn't be able to pee at all.

And I'd go into my cubicle and I'd lock myself in

and it was so much safer there.

Though wherever you are,

in the gents or in the ladies,

it's important no one hears you cry.

And here I am in Luigi's ladies and someone comes in to the one next door

and I think I mustn't cough

because I caused a commotion once when I coughed and someone said "There's a man in the loo!"

So I sit there very silent

and I hear their pee fall into in the water.

Mine doesn't do that. Mine hits the porcelain because I still pee through my penis.

I don't normally talk about such things.

because we are not our genitalia

and because these things are hard to talk about in front of a crowd of strangers.

And I so wish

I so wish they didn't matter.

I decide when I open the door I'm going to look in the mirror.

I might even do some make-up.

I don't often do it because I'm not very confident and I'm afraid I'll look ridiculous.

The woman who was peeing beside me is already at the mirror

and she's deftly doing her lipstick.

Looking at herself in the coldly appraising way women often use

when they want to impress a man

and are concerned with transforming themselves into the object of his desire.

She's had years of practice

I haven't had that

And so I often feel anxious

I'm afraid I'll look in the mirror and I'll see. . .

I'll see the boy

The boy I was or the boy that I was meant to be

Who looked in the mirror and didn't recognise who he saw

I take out my lipstick

And I paint my lips

And they are my lips

I may not like them much

I may want them to look like Angelina's

But they are mine.

And they never used to be.

PART THREE

1.

Dear John.

No wonder you're so angry!

Oh look at you.

Eighteen years old

Trying so hard to be normal

But normal was never who you were

And I was with you all along.

But you couldn't have known that, my loved one

For you were trapped in horizontal time

Where one damned thing comes after another

And it feels like there is no escaping

Because linear time belongs to the straight world

To the world of the school room and the workplace

Theatre belongs to a different time

Freedom comes from open time, from vertical time, queer time

That's where the power of this place comes from.

Always with you, my sweetheart

In the fifty years since you last stood on this kind of stage

And you are always in me and I was always in you

And this is the time

The brief time we have together —

2.

I spent a year in Spain when I was supposed to be studying.

But the dictatorship was collapsing and the universities were mostly closed.

So I spent the time trying to be a writer instead.

I filled notebook after notebook with poems and stories I was too shy to show anyone.

And when I came back home to the flat I was staying in

there was a beautiful girl on the sofa

wearing a black silk vintage skirt.

I loved her the minute I saw her and she loved me

Though we were both too scared to say it

Because rejection was more than we could both of us bear —

Oh Susie.

I don't know if I can bear to see you. It hurts.

At first we were so afraid to be together.

You wanted to make me happy. As I did you.

But what we did for each other was so much more.

Years later, my love, when I had to be seen by two psychiatrists

whose job was to tell me whether I was truly transsexual

and so whether I would qualify for surgery,

one of the questions they asked me was whether I was sexually aroused by wearing women's clothes.

Dear Susie: we couldn't have this conversation when you were alive because it only happened long after you were dead,

but in queer time

In queer time we can always and for ever talk together.

Those psychiatrists belonged to straight time

It was straight time paid their salaries

And when they asked me

Were you ever

Were you ever aroused by women's clothes

I said no.

Of course not.

I had read up all the symptoms

I knew what I was supposed to be feeling

And that if I said yes

I could have been classified as a fetishist

And so might have been refused surgery.

But I was lying.

And I know, my love, you and I were both taught it's a sin to tell a lie.

But how can it be a sin to lie when your life is called into question.

The thing is, dear, in those lonely days

Those days before I met you

Those days when I thought I would always be alone

I never wanted to make love to an attractive woman:

I wanted to *be* that woman

And that was enough to keep me turned on for ever —

And when I tried to be normal

I attempted to lose that

And lost myself as well.

You know, my dearest, the strange thing was, I never wanted to be you

I loved you

You were the most beautiful person in the whole wide world

And I wanted to make love to you more than anything

And I couldn't

I was dead inside

You were so patient and we tried so hard. . .

And then, for my twenty-second birthday, you gave me a half tab of acid

And the world . . . the world is expanding

The world is growing bigger and bigger

And smaller and smaller at the same time

And I bounce up and down on the bed

Up and down

Up and down

And I'm flying

I'm flying away on great white wings

It's so beautiful

I'm utterly entranced by the cracks in the floorboards

And I look in the mirror

And at first I see nothing. I must be a vampire!

And then I see a skull that laughs at me

But I am not afraid.

And then the skull becomes

The most beautiful woman

In a gorgeous silk dress

And I can't take my eyes off her

Because I know this woman:

I know this woman as I know myself

I am her and she is me and we are both in this together.

And this goes on for hours and hours and hours and hours

And then it's over

And a few more weeks go past and

Something happens and I find my erection

And we make the most amazing love together

And then for the very first time

I experience orgasm.

I'm twenty-two years old and it is amazing and amazing and
the best thing is that the feeling it gives me is the same feeling
I get from being dressed as a woman and that makes me think
it's not so terrible a thing after all.

Susie loves me and I love Susie

And the world is opening out

And I feel sexy

I feel very sexy

Look at my body!

Look at my hair!

Here I'm beautiful

Here I'm free

3.

I dream of a bridge

I'm fifty-two years old and I dream of a bridge across a chasm
in the mountains

A motorway bridge with two carriageways

And the one I'm on has come to a sudden end

I'm looking down over the jagged edges

Down into the deep fathomless darkness

And I know my life has come to an end.

That morning I'd gone to work as a university professor

And I'd looked at the timetable

I'd looked at the timetable and I couldn't understand it

University professors should be able to understand timetables

But I can't

I just can't

And I start crying.

I start crying and I cannot stop.

A kind colleague says:

Sometimes we break our leg

And it doesn't work any more.

It needs to rest.

And sometimes it happens our brain doesn't work any more

And we need to rest.

Go home. Go home.

And I did —

And it was that night I had that dream

Of the bridge.

And I looked and I saw

There was another carriageway

Another path across the chasm

What I had to do was stumble

Over some rubble and some broken rocks

And then the road went on.

4.

Hello John.

Your daughter took these photographs.

I know what it was.

You wanted someone to photograph you who loved you

And whom you loved

Someone to record the moment

Someone to bear witness.

For years and years I'd wanted to escape

Wanted to escape myself and keep living as a man

I'd tell everyone what mattered

What mattered as a man

Was that I came to terms with the woman inside me —

That all men do.

Come to terms with the woman inside us

The woman we've been taught to detest and to despise

And learn to love her still living as a man.

But she was too strong for me. She was tearing me apart.

You never knew you were a handsome man.

You always thought yourself so ugly.

You hung on

You hung on because you could not believe it was possible

that you could ever live as a woman.

And Susie

loved and needed you as a man and couldn't bear to lose you.

My love you know I never meant to cause you pain.

And then you started dying, Susie.

Brain tumour. You knew. You knew.

By this time I've heard a voice that's told me the woman in me is wholly good

and I'm committed now, totally committed to letting her out into the light:

but we both have so much work to do.

Dying is such hard work.

She faces it with courage and a kind of joyous laughter

that even in her torment is never fully stilled.

I'm holding onto her trying to stop her slipping away.

But she's going and I can't stop her and I don't know if I can bear it but I know I will.

We're like a couple in a weather thing. She will go into the dark and I —

I will come out into the light.

Goodbye Susie. Goodbye. Goodbye.

Silence.

I had a dear friend about that time,

Another university professor

The one who knew about town planning

Very eminent in their field

The one the doctor said wasn't serious and so they refused to help her.

She was someone whose shame was so extreme

She never could come out in her public life

Someone whose true life — whose woman's life —

Mostly happened behind closed doors.

And who finally drank herself to death.

Before she went she said:

There comes a time when you can't go on

You have to choose

Between living as a woman

Or dying as a man.

Oh Jo. You wanted to live. You always did.

You were the boy with burning eyes.

Silence.

Many of us disdain our former selves.

Many of us say: That wasn't me.

I want to remove him from the record.

But I won't do that.

I'm proud of you.

Dear John.

Proud you lived through all your pain

And still loved someone. And were loved in return.

Proud you and he and she brought up your amazing daughters.

Proud you found your voice and learnt to write.

Proud of all those plays.

Proud of the years of tears and laughter.

It was so hard for you leaving John behind.

But it was time to go.

Goodbye John. Goodbye. Goodbye.

Silence.

Soon after Susie died I started to feel frightened.

I couldn't understand why I was so constantly in a state of terror.

Cold sweat, sick in the stomach, weak in the knees, heart beating horribly fast.

I went to the doctor and she sent me to A&E.

I was lying on a trolley and couldn't go anywhere

and a group of doctors came to look at me and one said

"this fifty-five-year-old woman"

and he meant me.

And I looked at my wristband

and it said 'F' for female.

I know if they'd treated me as male I wouldn't have survived.

The surgeon said: this is when I give you an injection to stop your heart beating but don't worry, we'll connect you to machines to keep you alive.

And they did that:

but I was dead five hours while he put in the little plastic ring

to mend the broken valve that meant my heart was bleeding

and now that I'm alive I feel like I've been reborn.

It's a very simple thing to have your testicles removed —

just a little surgery to stop one's body producing male hormone.

It took me just three days to recover.

And soon after that I was cycling through a forest in France

in my jeans and my t-shirt and my hair in a mess

and the sun was shining, it was a beautiful afternoon

and I passed an old lady who was doing her garden.

We caught each other's eye and we smiled.

And she said: Bonjour madame.

5.

There's very little of my mother left.

But I got a postcard once.

On one side there's a picture of the sights of London.

There's Buckingham Palace

There's St Paul's Cathedral

There's Tower Bridge.

She wrote:

Paddington. Tuesday.

Just going to catch our train.

Many well dones about going!

Much love Mummy.

To RJ Clifford, Forres, Swanage, Dorset.

Dear mummy

I know you were proud of me because that day you'd packed me off to boarding school

and I hadn't made a fuss.

And you know, dear mummy, I still don't. Mostly

don't make a fuss. I just get on with things.

I've written ninety plays. This is the ninety-first! You'd be proud of me.

Wrote them partly because it was the only way I knew to make a living

And partly to convince myself and the world

That I really do have the right to exist.

You worried about me, I know,

You were afraid I'd turn out to be a pansy.

A pansy. As you called it.

I'd call it queer.

And it's true, mother. It's all true.

But you don't need to worry. I'm all right.

I wish you'd met Susie. I wish you'd met our daughters.

They're successful grown up women now and they both have lovely men.

And I have a grandson.

When he sees me his face lights up

And he calls me grandma.

Did you think you'd failed me, mummy,

because you couldn't make me into a proper man?

You never failed me. You loved me.

And this is who I'm meant to be.

There is a story in a book that we've all heard

About Eve who is the mother of us all.

She lives in a garden and one day we'll all be there

We'll all be there in love and joy and we won't know shame.

Part of us is there already

You and me and Susie and my mum.

And on that day we too will have no shame.

Silence.

This is me,

I am Jo,

and I've lived a long time now.

Sixty-seven years.

I've fathered two children. I adore them.

My two wonderful daughters and my grandson too.

I loved a woman for thirty-three years.

I know what it is to be a man;

I know what it is to be a woman, too.

I have no time for shame.

Sister death is knocking at my body's door.

Sister death is waiting

Just around the corner of the street

Or maybe just before my eyes.

Maybe it will still be years.

But she will come.

She'll know her time.

And on that day I will embrace my death,

Embrace her o so gladly

And fly like a swan on great white wings,

Fly like a swan into the unknown darkness,

Like a swan singing.

End.